# Ten Steps To Success

# In Network Marketing

A practical guide for people dealing

professionally with the MLM system

David A. Hill

# INTRODUCTION

Welcome to a ten steps guide how to succeed in network marketing.

If you are reading this, it means that you would like to succeed in this distribution of products and services.

With all my heart I wish you that you succeed like many millions of people in the world.

Consider this guide as a success diary. Write down everything that comes to your mind.

Each page should be written with reflections and thoughts.

In the place of the dotted lines, insert the name of the company with which you cooperate.

Therefore, let's do it. I wish you to achieve your goals.

David

### Welcome to the world

..........................................(write here the name of company you cooperate with).

Till the end of your life you will buy products that ....................
.......................... have in its offer.

As a consumer you will make extra money for commercial chains, producers or stores - without reciprocity, these companies will not share part of the money with you. You are getting poorer - they are getting richer. You spend money irretrievably, doing shopping becomes your expense, cash goes one way only - to the producer and intermediaries.

As a conscious prosumer ............................. - you can make money and get rich when doing shopping. You become a partner of the producer and you benefit from constant discounts on products.

If you help ............................. to advertise products, gain market, win leaders over, you can get unlimited financial benefits from global turnover of whole company!

The marketing plan gives you great opportunities to create passive income, a great career, and what it follows - stability and security for your family and for you.

# STEP 1

## WHY IS IT WORTH TAKING SERIOUSLY THE CHANCE OF COOPERATION - WHAT PROBLEMS DOES THE COOPERATION SOLVE?

We live in times where contemporary economy gives everyone a chance for financial stability, full independence, additional income or full prosperity.

............................ acts in the system of creating your own business organization, where you can work out passive income, which is so important in this world.

Imagine that you are working on building your own organization of clients and business partners for 5-7 years, and after that time your network is developing on its own and you receive dividends from the fact that you gave it impetus and a beginning.

Such a system of earning gives freedom.

Taking this business seriously will result in you starting to consciously solve life problems with this project.

Lack of time, money, prospects, freedom, development and health is a key factor in how to perceive cooperation.

The changing market conditions, the lack of stable employment, and high competition in businesses mean that a professional approach to the model ............................. motivates you to focus and to act maturely and seriously.

Think about your future, what do you see  doing the same thing for the past 5-10 years?

Please have a look at the circles below, building consciously a business organization can save you from these below.

A breakthrough in life begins when you make the decision to start this business model at a hundred percent and when you act seriously as a business model when building your organization.

You have a plan, goals, vision, you know exactly what problems you will solve thanks to this business and you lose yourself in unbridled action.

## SUCCESS MEANS RIGHTS, WISDOM IS TO PUT THEM INTO ACTION

Your life depends on you, it's up to you what you will do with your time. ............................ operates in a system that can give you abundance, prosperity, financial and personal success. The system is automation, scale, levers, product, entry time, people.

Job posistion is not a system, business is not a system. There will be no freedom from such forms of earning money.

## SCALE - 100% OF THE POPULATION

Everyone on the earth uses the products of the first need. Therefore the scale is unlimited. Everyone can be your client or business partner. The scale of building a business in ...................................... is unlimited - the whole world.

## CONTROL - YOUR COMPANY

The main rule how to become wealthy is that the control of action must be on your side. In ............................ you decide how you act, with whom, where, how seriously. You earn proportionally to the turnover created by the shopping of your network.

On a standard full-time job you do not decide on the fate of the company. In a conventional business a lot of external factors such as town, street, weather, regulations, competition, etc. decide about your success or failure.

## PRODUCT PASSIVENESS - THE HIGHEST

The product's passivity ratio will determine the financial and repeatable success - passive income. ........................................ is a producer of quickly consumable first need products. What does it mean? It means that every customer or business partner needs to buy it again, what it follows that commission will be charged. You create future passive income from repetitive products by building a network of regular customers.

## AUTOMATION - THE PROJECT DEVELOPS ITSELF

In this business model the best thing is that you can make new partners emancipated through the recruitment of new partners, trainings and support for the team.

Thanks to that they create groups of clients or teams of leaders on their own. After a few years of conscious work, the organization lives with its own momentum and life, creating more and more turnovers and new recruitment's.

Automation is the key to freedom and financial independence, which is why this distribution model gives you unlimited possibilities of development and income.

## UNLIMITED LEVERS - PEOPLE, INTERNET, CONTACTS

When you go through life alone, you are doomed to mediocrity. When you build a group of clients, leaders, consultants - you start to use the incredible capabilities of other people. Recommending new clients, recruitment of new business partners, devoting time by people in your network, their acquaintance.

Levers that occur in business ..............................., make that you can achieve great financial success, great momentum – even international, acquiring new clients and business partners outside your community.

Look forward to the future optimistically, plan what to do and see clearly where you see yourself in 3 years?

## YOU MUST HAVE STRONG ADVANTAGES IN ONE FINGER MARKETING NETWORK

What is unique in products ...................................................?

What is unique in the distribution system through marketing network? In what why it's different from a full-time job? From standard business?

What is unique in the marketing plan ...................................?

What makes it different?

## FIND MOTIVATION IN YOU AND STRENGTH FOR SERIOUS AND FOCUSED ACTION

What is at the end of your path, at the end of your plan for life, if you don't change anything in action, approach?

What is waiting for you in 3, 5 or 10 years if you continue to do the same?

Why do you want to promote products ....................................?

What is your mission?

What financial "pain" do you see in people and in yourself in order to make a serious decision about active action with ...........................................?

(What problems do you solve thanks to this project?)

What priority do you want to give to an action when building your income system with.............................................................? Why should it be important to you?

How seriously do you want to take this action?

How fast do you want to become an expert in this business? What will you do to become the expert?

 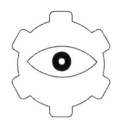

## VISION AND MEANING OF

## COMMITMENT

What is your important, specific reason to get involved seriously in the project ..........................?

What do you think, what amount of monthly income will satisfy you completely, provide security and let live a good life for your family and for you?

▫ Up to 1 000  ▫ Up to 3 000  ▫ Up to 5 000  ▫ Up to 15 000
▫Up to 25 000  ▫Up to 50 000 ▫ Up to 100 000 your currency.

What kind of life do you want to live thanks to your success with
............................. ...? (consider family, personal life,
relationship, finance, helping people, traveling, time for your
family, peacefulness, security, other areas of life important to you).



What is your plan for 3 months? Financial goal? ...................

What is your plan for 6 months? Financial goal? ...................

What is your plan for 12 months? Financial goal? ...................

What will you do to 3-5 years? Financial goal? ...................

| Your goals and dreams: | How much does it cost? |
|---|---|
| 1. ................................................... | ................................. |
| 2. ................................................... | ................................. |
| 3. ................................................... | ................................. |
| 4. ................................................... | ................................. |
| 5. ................................................... | ................................. |
| 6. ................................................... | ................................. |
| 7. ................................................... | ................................. |
| 8. ................................................... | ................................. |

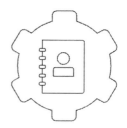

## CONTACT LIST

Professional building of personal network is an economics model which gives a new profession, good perspectives and control over your business.

Everyone has so called "pain" in life or work. That's why a leader who seriously treats cooperation shares information with everyone.

Prepare a quick contact list with people that you can help by showing a cooperation model with ...............................

Condition - do not judge anyone, do not decide for anyone, do not classify. Everyone misses something different. Some for better financial conditions, others for independence, peacefulness, free time, and others for career and success.

Date of meeting:

1. ............................... contact .................. ..................
2. ............................... contact .................. ..................
3. ............................... contact .................. ..................
4. ............................... contact .................. ..................
5. ............................... contact .................. ..................
6. ............................... contact .................. ..................
7. ............................... contact .................. ..................
8. ............................... contact .................. ..................
9. ............................... contact .................. ..................
10. ...........................contact .................. ..................
11. ...........................contact .................. ..................
12. ...........................contact .................. ..................
13. ...........................contact .................. ..................
14. ...........................contact .................. ..................
15. ...........................contact .................. ..................
16. ...........................contact .................. ..................
17. ...........................contact .................. ..................
18. ...........................contact .................. ..................
19. ...........................contact .................. ..................
20. ...........................contact .................. ..................
21. ...........................contact .................. ..................
22. ...........................contact .................. ..................
23. ...........................contact .................. ..................
24. ...........................contact .................. ..................

25. ...............................contact ...................  ..................
26. ...............................contact ...................  ..................
27. ...............................contact ...................  ..................
28. ...............................contact ...................  ..................
29. ...............................contact ...................  ..................
30. ...............................contact ...................  ..................
31. ...............................contact ...................  ..................
32. ...............................contact ...................  ..................
33. ...............................contact ...................  ..................
34. ...............................contact ...................  ..................
35. ...............................contact ...................  ..................
36. ...............................contact ...................  ..................
37. ...............................contact ...................  ..................
38. ...............................contact ...................  ..................
39. ...............................contact ...................  ..................
40. ...............................contact ...................  ..................
41. ...............................contact ...................  ..................
42. ...............................contact ...................  ..................
43. ...............................contact ...................  ..................
44. ...............................contact ...................  ..................
45. ...............................contact ...................  ..................
46. ...............................contact ...................  ..................
47. ...............................contact ...................  ..................
48. ...............................contact ...................  ..................
49. ...............................contact ...................  ..................
50. ...............................contact ...................  ..................

51. ...............................contact ...................  .....................
52. ...............................contact ...................  .....................
53. ...............................contact ...................  .....................
54. ...............................contact ...................  .....................
55. ...............................contact ...................  .....................
56. ...............................contact ...................  .....................
57. ...............................contact ...................  .....................
58. ...............................contact ...................  .....................
59. ...............................contact ...................  .....................
60. ...............................contact ...................  .....................
61. ...............................contact ...................  .....................
62. ...............................contact ...................  .....................
63. ...............................contact ...................  .....................
64. ...............................contact ...................  .....................
65. ...............................contact ...................  .....................
66. ...............................contact ...................  .....................
67. ...............................contact ...................  .....................
68. ...............................contact ...................  .....................
69. ...............................contact ...................  .....................
70. ...............................contact ...................  .....................
71. ...............................contact ...................  .....................
72. ...............................contact ...................  .....................
73. ...............................contact ...................  .....................
74. ...............................contact ...................  .....................
75. ...............................contact ...................  .....................
76. ...............................contact ...................  .....................

77. ..........................contact .................. ..................

78. ..........................contact .................. ..................

79. ..........................contact .................. ..................

80. ..........................contact .................. ..................

81. ..........................contact .................. ..................

82. ..........................contact .................. ..................

83. ..........................contact .................. ..................

84. ..........................contact .................. ..................

85. ..........................contact .................. ..................

86. ..........................contact .................. ..................

87. ..........................contact .................. ..................

88. ..........................contact .................. ..................

89. ..........................contact .................. ..................

90. ..........................contact .................. ..................

91. ..........................contact .................. ..................

92. ..........................contact .................. ..................

93. ..........................contact .................. ..................

94. ..........................contact .................. ..................

95. ..........................contact .................. ..................

96. ..........................contact .................. ..................

97. ..........................contact .................. ..................

98. ..........................contact .................. ..................

99. ..........................contact .................. ..................

100. ..........................contact .................. ..................

## LEARN THE PRODUCT AND BUSINESS PRESENTATION AS SOON AS POSSIBLE

# 1 WAY

If you want to be a distributor - consultant, learn how to present the unique features, advantages and benefits of ……………………….. products as soon as possible.

Build a customer network and earn from a margin 25%, also from cash back system. Attractive product prices and the best warehouses in the world will result in almost 100% of your friends' database becoming customers.

Every day set up a meeting and present …………………………….. offer, your goal is to get the biggest turnover in the shortest possible time.

Attention! Always take orders from customers, so that you can help your products ……………………… their friends. Thanks to that, you constantly expand your market and increase turnover, and this gives you unlimited commissions.

# 2 WAY

If you are building a group, an organization - learn to make presentations on your own as soon as possible and register the first 4-5 people. At the beginning, the first presentations can be done by your guardian if you have never acted in such a business model.

It's important to go directly to the action, because that's the only way business is done. Unrestrained action counts.

## SETTING UP YOUR GROUP'S OR CUSTOMER'S MEETINGS

Each person registered in the system sets up meetings of his friends with you, for example 3 meetings per day (e.g. every 1 hour) in order to register 4-5 people to the system as soon as possible.

The aim is to make the first position of the newly registered person. Only you or you together with your leader are preparing a meeting for new people.

If you are a consultant and you deal with sales, and the client wants to help you meet with his friends, make an offer to this person, for example sales margins for the organizer or suggest registration to

the system and deepening the knowledge about the
................................. model.

## TEACHING A PRESENTATION OF NEWLY REGISTERED PARTNERS

Minimum 2 times a month, one day (e.g. on Saturday), you teach the presentation all the new people or your helper/leader does it. If the business is intended to develop quickly - teach the presentation each person who wants to create a group and wants to make more money.

## CHECK, WATCH THESE STEPS OF THE SYSTEM, MOTIVATE, DEVELOP YOURSELF AND THE TEAM FURTHER

Basic principles of each distributor and leaders:

**1.** Uses products personally - is reliable, recommends something that he knows personally.

**2.** Recommends products - broadens knowledge and market.

**3.** Builds an organization - creates his own personal network and has influence on its development taking benefits from network's turnover.

## LOOK

- You are a network entrepreneur, so the appearance at meetings and presentations must be businesslike and neat. You show respect for the other person and create a professional image of yourself, you make a good impression and show that you treat your project seriously.
- Clean business shoes, nice nails, ironed shirt, freshness and perfumes are the basis of a good impression. Of course, a wide smile.

## ATTITUDE

- An absolute basis in this industry is a positive attitude towards the product, company, branch and marketing plan. Optimistic planning of your goals should trigger enthusiasm and joy in action. Therefore, think over everything carefully and organize great meetings, telephone conversations, training's and your actions in Internet.

## ATTITUDE AND APPROACH

- To make it possible to make your dreams come true with ................................................................, it's worth to have a professional approach and a strong attitude. Always have a goal in front of your eyes, do your duties every day and move forward whenever you can. You are on a path that can lead you to financial independence. Therefore, treat the subject max seriously and focus on persevering action.

# ACTION PLAN - DESIGN THE WAY TO YOUR DREAM LIFE

Planning creates a focus on long-term action, which is the basis for achieving greater business successes.

When do I plan the first level? Date: …………………..
- How do I know that I have made a mature, irrevocable decision and is it forever?

When do I plan a second level? Date: ………………….....
- What I will do to achieve it:

When do I plan the third level? Date: …….……………..
- What I will do to achieve it:

When do you plan the fourth level? Date: …………………………..

- What I will do to achieve it:

When do I plan the fifth level? Date: …………………...………..

- What I will do to achieve it:

When do you plan the sixth level? Date: …………………………..

- What I will do to achieve it:

When do I plan the seventh level? Date: ……………...………..…..

• How will this level change me and my future?

When do I plan the eighth level? Date: …………………...………..

- How am I ready for this success?

When do I plan the last level? Date: …………………………..

- What will I do with this money, rank and freedom?

What will the final decision look like that you will completely lose yourself in action?

# STEP 4

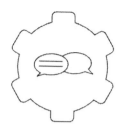

## LEARNING TO INVITE

An invitation to a meeting is a key activity of the entrepreneur. This is the first contact of your candidate to work with your business. The phone call is a "test" for the person you are calling to, test to check if he is ready for action and mature in order to get involved into something serious.

**ATTENTION.**

- The invitation is used only to arrange a meeting.
- On the phone you do not tell the name of the company, what the company does and what produces, how it makes money - you do not sell anything. You just have to book a meeting time.
- On the phone you do not use the word "MLM" and name of products.

## EXAMPLE

- "Good morning Paul, how are you?"
You're listening.
- "Paul, there's a new, cool theme, unique in every way, what are you doing on Thursday at 20.00?"
You're listening.
- "I'll come to you. Write it down."

## HOW TO TEST SOMEONE

- "Are you interested in money? Yes? I will come to you, there is a good theme."
- "Will you find space for an additional 2-3 thousand in the wallet every month?"
- "Do you know someone who needs a few thousand more in the wallet?"

## ANY QUESTIONS LIKE

- "What is it?"
- "What's going on?"
- "Is it MLM?"
- "How much money should I pay?" etc.

## YOU ALWAYS ANSWER

- "I will tell you everything when we meet, trust me, this is a hit! You'll see it yourself."

## REMEMBER

You have an idea, product, plan, help, training and system - and people are looking for more time, money, peace, health, etc.

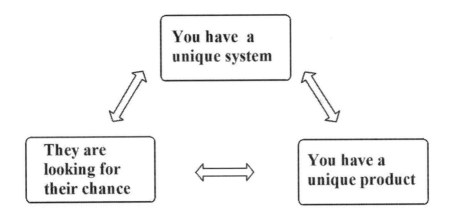

## FINALIZATION OF BUSINESS MEETINGS - A PILL

If you know that you are in search of people with leadership potential, please do not use words:
- "Register"
- "Sign in"
- "Buy cheaper."

## REGISTRATION ITSELF DOES NOT CHANGE THEIR LIFE, WILL NOT BRING SECURITY

Inspire them to build an independent source of passive income.

## ALWAYS BREAK THE MEETING FIRMLY AND CONCRETELY

- "Do you see any reason why not to build the business with me today?"

- "Let's start great action. Are you in?"

- "What do you like the most in this project?"

- "How much do you like this theme in scale 1 to 10?"

- "After what I showed you, do you see any reason not to explore the subject deeper?"

If someone is ready to start cooperation, do not impose the registration method, just ask a question:

- "What budget do you want to start - any purchase, small bundle or professionally - a large bundle?"

**Do not register people without shopping** - you will destroy respect for the company, and this person will quickly give up because there was no investment "pain" in business, so this person will not care to act seriously.

## THE CANON OF GOOD LEADER PRACTICES - A RECIPE FOR SUCCESS

### PRESENTATIONS

- "Sylvia, let's get to the reason of my visit. I met people who implement a good project, before I go into details, please tell me"

- "What do you do? How are you living?"

- "How do you handle financially? How at work?"

- "How do you see your prospects in your current job / business?"

- "Would you like a few thousand more for your family?"

## BUILD A RANGE OF MEETING

- "If you would earn enough to make you feel safe and fulfilled, you could afford to save money and have an ideal life - how much would it be?"

- "By doing what you do now, will you ever be able to earn so much?"

## COLLEAGUES

**1.** Stage of talks, relations.
**2.** Proceed to the essence of the meeting.

- "Listen, let me get to the bottom of today's meeting. I am your colleague/friend for many years and you know that I wish you well.

That's why I am here today because I discovered/found fantastic project and interesting people. I made the decision that I would present it to you. Look at the details and see if this theme can bring something good to your life and will help your family."

**3.** Stage of showing presentation / movie / webinar / etc.

## LEADERS, OTHER MARKETING SPECIALISTS

- "Mike, I know that you are active in your business and you are really involved, but I want to ask you an important question.
If there was a topic that would start the action now, with great products of everyday use, therefore an unlimited operating market, great prices, training and development support, and you could be in the initial phase and thanks to that you would have the entire market to take over, which will bring excellent commissions, would you be interested to go with me for coffee?" (if invitation)


or


- "... would you be interested in serious 100% involvement in the operation?"

# THE PACE OF ACTION - 90 DAYS FROM THE MOMENT OF MAKING DECISION IS THE KEY TO SUCCESS

Success loves speed, so prepare a good plan of action, get ready and start.

Aim - register 20 people in a month or as many as you can.

You work on your own from the beginning or do you need help? Arrange it and prepare help - introductory person, leader, mentor, who will you ask for help:

..........................................................................................

---

**PREPARATION**

- Write how much you care:

..........................................................................................

..........................................................................................

- Revise classes and empty the calendar - remove everything you can, which certainly does not lead you on the path of financial independence.

- Eliminate distractions - you start the project of life.

- Convince yourself 100% for products and serious action.

- Go all the way (go big) - you have everything you dream about to gain! Nothing to lose!

---

# FIRST TEN DAYS

- 100% effort and compression of action.
- You call everyone with enthusiasm and from everywhere: in a car, after lunch, in the morning, in the evening, you do as many presentations as you maximally can.
- Skype, one for one, webinar, meetings, phone call (go into it in dark), FB, YT.

# SECOND TEN DAYS

- You do follow up – you close it enthusiastically, full of energy and passion.
- You keep the contact, you take orders and fire!
- You register and immediately you do presentations with new registered people.

# THIRD TEN DAYS

- You finish, you come back to these which are not decided yet.

- You keep the contact, you take orders and you go on enthusiastically and with passion.

- You put people in the system, webinars, you all start regional meetings and meeting at home, 3-10 days of duplication with others.

Organize minimum 50 meetings as fast as possible.

 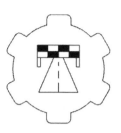

# CONSIDER ................................................
# SERIOUSLY - IT'S THE WAY TO THE GOAL!

To make business move towards dreams, you have to do something for your project every day. You must find time if you think about financial independence from building a network.

Plan: when do you work? When do you have private classes? When do you want to spend time with your family?

In the remaining time, plan when you will work on building your freedom.

| HR | MON | TUE | WED | THU | FRI | SAT | SUN |
|---|---|---|---|---|---|---|---|
| 6 AM | | | | | | | |
| 7 AM | | | | | | | |
| 8 AM | | | | | | | |
| 9 AM | | | | | | | |
| 10 AM | | | | | | | |
| 11 AM | | | | | | | |
| 12 AM | | | | | | | |
| 1 PM | | | | | | | |
| 2 PM | | | | | | | |
| 3 PM | | | | | | | |
| 4 PM | | | | | | | |
| 5 PM | | | | | | | |
| 6 PM | | | | | | | |
| 7 PM | | | | | | | |
| 8 PM | | | | | | | |
| 9 PM | | | | | | | |

How many hours a week do you want/can you to spend on meetings and presentations? ………………..

How many presentations do you want to show per week?

………………..

Which days you can fill the calendar with meetings:

………………..

How many people do you want to register per week?

………………..

How many business partners do you want to join in a week?

………………..

How many unknown people a week do you want to contact on FB or in your life? ………………..

When do you start working with a professional approach?
Date: ………………..

**Setting first presentation for you**, date: ……………………………
How many people: ………………
**Setting second presentation for you**, date: ……………………………
How many people: ………………
**Setting third presentation for you**, date: ……………………………
How many people: ………………

## THE CANON OF GOOD LEADER PRACTICES - A RECIPE FOR SUCCESS

Checklist of the leader - check what you do and look after these tasks also for others in your team.

CHECK OUT NEW REGISTERED PARTICIPANTS EVERY DAY, SEND THEM BY EMAIL:

- Business presentation and career path.
- Product presentation.
- Links with webinars and schedule of training.
- Call and say hello, show that you are ready to help and get closer contact.
- Check if recruitment and sale meetings – contracts are planned.
- Send training movies, leader's canons.
- "Ten steps guide" implementation up to 48 hours after registration - follow up (as soon as possible).
- Prepare plan of action, set goals, build strong motivation inside yourself.
- Remind other regularly about webinars, trainings, meetings – call, send mails, talk.

## MANAGE AND LOOK AFTER THE TEAM:

- Send email reminding about webinars, workshops, trainings, meetings, conferences.
- Promote leaders, creators and mentors working.
- Promote training's, conferences, workshops - this is where man becomes a leader.
- For people who want to act – prepare so called "meeting marathon" 3-4 business and sales meetings.
- Do "follow up" - as often as possible introduce a man into business, make ten steps (phone call, skype).
- Build a circle of people with whom you have a personal contact on the phone phone and via email.
- Key liaison, leaders - be regularly at meetings and trainings

## DEVELOP YOURSELF ALL THE TIME:

- Every day for 30 minutes read books about personal development, business, network marketing and leadership.
- Take notes, gain knowledge, draw conclusions from webinars, training's, movies, meetings.
- Go to training's, take as many people as possible to workshops, conferences, etc.

## CHECKLIST OF EVERYDAY LEADER'S ACTIVITIES:

- Business meetings.

- Sales and product meeting.

- An implementation meeting, training team.

- The training to empower the leaders, the team.

- Own sale - building your customer network.

- Building the list - new contacts, taking orders, networking.

- Building a personal brand and authority - an article for blog, funpage in Facebook.


**- JUST ACT!**

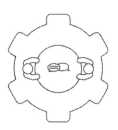

## BUSINESS MEETINGS

No idea will develop without meetings. It's thanks to meetings that people are introduced to the product, accounting plan and vision.

You can organize them personally, via Skype at a distance, even being abroad, webinars, home meetings for more people or regional meetings. Of course there are also workshops and training's and events for a larger number of people.

This business is only proceeded with meetings - because you get a commission for advertising the company and its products.

In order for the business to move forward, it is worth to organize minimum 5/10 meetings a week or operate in the system of 3 meetings per week x 3 people at the meeting.

If someone organizes less, then it means that he has not understood the idea and perspective that action in this business model gives him. Fast results are 2-3 meetings a day without break for 90 days. It gives you a powerful momentum and the results are enormous.

A person who needs concrete results, sets the action target for 3 months from the start and registration.

## HOW TO START MEETINGS?

From getting to know the life and financial situation of a given person or family, ask questions and just listen:

- "How is your life?"

- "How are you at work? / How business?"

- "What are your prospects for the future while doing what you are still doing?"

- "What pension do you expect?"

- "At what level do you earn today? Up to 3 - 5 thousand? More?"

- "If you could earn enough to make you feel safe, and be able to look at the future securely, how much would it be?"

**A.** When having conversation – you are listening to the "pain" of life, work, everyday life. Financial problems, underestimation at work, lack of time, tiredness, routine, competition or costs - hardly anyone has a wonderful life.

**B.** After listening to understanding the human situation, go to a paper presentation, presentation from laptop, show a movie or simply draw a system of ......................................on the sheet of paper.

**C.** You always close the meeting with a concrete question about decisions:

- "Do you see any reason not to start building this business from today?"

- "Do you see any reason to create a team together and build a future based on this project?"

**D.** You register a person and go through this training with him and organize a meeting for his friends.
You provide her materials, presentations, links, you teach him shopping and you support him.

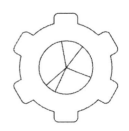

# STEP 7

## STEREOTYPES - WHAT YOU NEED TO KNOW BEFORE YOU START

Facts are facts, and there are often false opinions about this distribution model.

Prepare yourself in terms of content when you talk.

They can ask you on the phone:

- "What is this meeting for which you invite me?"
- "Trust me, when we meet, I will tell you everything, too much talking on the phone for such serious topic."

- "Is it MLM?"
- "No, it's a system ................................, original manufacturer's system, 100% of people earn! Hit! I will tell you everything when we meet."

- "How much should I pay for it? Do I have to pay for it anyway?"
- "Trust me, you do not have to pay anything, if we meet, I will tell you everything."

- "What do I have to drag?"
- "Stop fooling around, what does it mean to drag? If we meet, I will tell you everything."

- "Is this a pyramid system? Is it some kind of chain letter again?"
- "Do not be ridiculous, please."

- "I do not have time for any unimportant things."
- "I do not either, that's why I'm calling you, so that you will look in the calendar and plan your time exactly."

- "I do not have any money for any business."
- "That's why I'm calling you so that you finally start to have money!"

- "If you do not tell me, I will not come."
- "So do not come. Who you have me for? I want to rob you? Deceive? How long do you know me?"

- "Give me peace of mind with those of your businesses where no one makes money."
- "And here you are wrong - here 100% people earn. When we meet, you will see it."

- "I've already taken part in something like this."
- "No, you have never been in something like this, trust me."

- "I have already lost a lot of money in such businesses, I do not want to start anything like this again."
- "I know, I understand, that's why I call you, so that you will see how to regain it with interest, look at the calendar."

- "I will not be drawn into anything."
- "I also do not, so check the calendar and see how this topic can help you in life."

- "I know what is going on in this kind of businesses."
- "If you knew, you would earn over 10 000 a month minimum, so check the calendar and find one hour."

 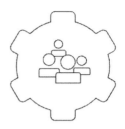

# TEAM

Going through life alone, we cannot do much. Lever that occurs in this model is the greatest secret to achieving success. Other people's time, contacts and finances, commitment and attention, their authority and motivation - work for you and their benefit.

Cooperating together, you are gaining a profit. You help them, you join them in the system, products, training's, you give them support and help at the beginning - and their turnover also supports you. Everyone has benefits from it.

## TEAM DEVELOPMENT STRATEGY IS THE SELECTION OF THE RIGHT PEOPLE:

1. Search for builders who want to be active and act seriously.

2. Search for people ready to do business tasks.

3. Look for entrepreneurial people who want to improve their life.

4. Search for people who are self-reliant or ready for education.

5. Search for people with a vision - for years of active building.

6. Search for people who are ready to provide information on meetings.

7. Search for people who can be preserving and systematic.

## IDEAL CANDIDATES FOR FUTURE LEADERS:

- Friendly.
- Self-confident.
- Ready to act.
- Ambitious.
- Mature to large finances.
- Motivated.
- Organized.
- With self-discipline.
- Ready to act on its own account.

Where will you look for business partners? How you want to do it? How will you tell them?

## MATURE TO THE CHANCE YOU GOT AND TO SERIOUS TEAM BUILDING

What is your current picture of yourself as a leader? Try to describe it.

..............................................................................................

..............................................................................................

What can you change? Who do you want to become as a responsible team leader?

..............................................................................................

..............................................................................................

What words will you use to describe yourself as a leader?

..........................................................................................................

..........................................................................................................

What can you add to the description to be positive, build a strong image in your own eyes?

..........................................................................................................

..........................................................................................................

Do your images and words support your self-confidence? Do they give you belief and energy? What do you have to change when it comes to thinking about yourself as a leader?

..........................................................................................................

..........................................................................................................

How do people perceive you as a leader, expert? What do you need to change to be reliable, consistent?

..........................................................................................................

..........................................................................................................

## LEADERSHIP MISSION

What mission do you want to have / what mission do you have to be satisfied as a leader?

..................................................................................................

..................................................................................................

What problems do you want to solve with the project ....................

............................ and what problem do you want to solve with your actions?

..................................................................................................

..................................................................................................

Why do you want to become a professional leader of your life?

..................................................................................................

..................................................................................................

Why do you consider this role of life important to you?

..................................................................................................

..................................................................................................

How does this way of life affect your sense of life and real happiness feeling?

..................................................................................................

..................................................................................................

On what values do you want to base your action as a leader?

..............................................................................................

..............................................................................................

Your declaration of the leadership mission is an agreement only with you. If you are ready to be steadfast in accordance with the written guidelines, sign it.

.............................................

## LEADER'S MENTALITY

Being a leader is making choices and difficult decisions. Nobody is born a leader - you simply make a choice and change your approach and attitude to building a business. Being a recommendation businessman is making an irrevocable decision on unrestrained action to enter the path of independence.

**TO BECOME A LEADER - YOU NEED TO FOLLOW 10 RULES**

**1.** Act actively and systematically despite of initial anxiety and stress.

**2.** Stop expecting, be passive and dependent on others. You are independent and active.

**3.** Contact people in various ways and channels, and present them a ............................................ model.

**4.** Register people and lead them, teaching them what you already know, build relations.

**5.** Inspiring, motivating the team and yourself for action and effort - which is very profitable.

**6.** Become a model for yourself and others. You give a good example of how you work.

**7.** You realize your goals and plans and you help others to realize them too.

**8.** You are brave, focused, consistent internally - you know why you do it and do your own thing.

**9.** You have goals, dreams and a vision to which you are going to and you take other people with you.

**10.** You are tenacious and consistent, you are stubborn and a strong will.

How can you help yourself to become a professional leader? Who can you ask for help? What books should you read? Which trainings should you take part in?

As the leader, who do you want to be? How do you want to think? How to act? How to serve your team?

## LEADER'S TASKS

**1.** He is taking care of a team, he keeps the positive bonds, he is interested in people in the team.

**2.** He trains his team, creates conditions for their development - all the time regularly.

**3.** He keeps contact with the best leaders, supports the weaker ones, serves people with knowledge and support.

**4.** Accompanies them for the first weeks and months, prepares presentations for their friends. Teaches, develops.

**5.** Promotes workshops, trainings, events, webinars and the .....................................education system.

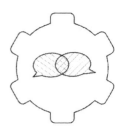

# STEP 10

## BREAKING DOWN OBJECTIONS AND NEGOTIATIONS

Many people have a false view of the team building industry. That's why always base on facts, listen patiently and let them talk. Never explain yourself, do not quarrel, do not enter disputes, but ask, ask and ask again:

- "What facts do you base this statement on?"

- "What is your personal experience in building teams that you give such opinion?"

If someone tells you that he was in such businesses and it does not work, then calmly ask:

- "What exactly were you doing that you did not earn?"

- "What exactly does not work in this business?"

Many people "burned" at MLM, failed to succeed, so you have to understand them, put yourself into somebody's shoes and look from their point of view:

- "I understand you. Probably if I was in your place, it would also not work for me, I would not have gained the result, but it is different here. .......................................... is not MLM - here everyone earns, everyone gets money. We have a training system, webinars, unique products, books and support materials. You join me and I will not leave you, we will work together and we will go through this together."

**OBJECTION:**

- "I do not have time."
- "That's why I am here for you, so that you will finally find time!"

- "I have no money."
- "That's why I am here for you, so that you will finally have money."

- "I do not have time for such businesses."
- "Listen, what do you have no time for? Doing what you're still doing, what are you expecting? What pension? What chance do you have to get your business going again? Are you able to double your income this year? How many years do you work in your life? How much money did you save? If you do not have a system, you work for survival, not for peace and security."

- "I do not have friends to do such a business"
- "You live on the moon? How many people do you have on your phone list? Do not you have Facebook? You will always be able to meet people. It's an excuse."

- "No one will come in."
- "You have friends who have too much money? Time? How do you know, do you read the future?"

- "In this kind of businesses no one makes money."
- "You know all people? A million people in world are doing such projects, the turnover is over 3 billion. What do you think, who takes the commission?"

Technique and strategy of building bonds, uniting people.

If someone is sceptical, take over his point of view, always tell him:

- "I understand your objection, I was also like that, but I allowed myself to get to know the other side of the coin and I opened up to get to know another side." (and here tell him your story, knowledge, belief).

# WHEN ACTING, LEARN

Start is a strong decision supported on the action plan, but it is not worth to wait. Time is the only resource, the most valuable - which is never recoverable. Delaying conscious actions contributes to enormous losses that cannot be compensated.

**SET THE DATE OF THE FINAL DECISION:**

.......................................................................................

**HOW DO YOU KNOW THAT YOU HAVE MADE A SERIOUS DECISION?**

## CONCLUSION

Such a system as .......................................... has not been in the history of the recommendation economy yet. You can be part of something unique and wonderful and give families a plan to improve their financial lives for now and for the future.

## "IF 2-3 PEOPLE ARE UNITED IN A COMMON GOAL - EVERYTHING IS POSSIBLE."

So what will be your next step of action?

I believe that what you have inside yourself achieves all success, not an accounting program and a product. Only what is happening in your mind, heart and soul can make you a smiling and joyful wanderer through your life, who is going ahead, on the way passing some goals that he will achieve. But it is not these goals that will be the meaning of the journey, but just wandering your dream path - the everyday process.

## DO NOT GIVE UP, GOOD LUCK, DAVID.

Printed in Great Britain
by Amazon